New Leaves

Leah Engel

Presentation by *BookLeaf Publishing*

Web: www.bookleafpub.com

E-mail: info@bookleafpub.com

ISBN: 9789357440301

First edition 2023

I dedicate this book to my parents, sister,
and my loving husband.

Warm

A ray of sun glitters on the sand
While I glow with the sensation of your hand in
my hand
Eyes gleaming and smiles beaming,
We are home in each other's love

A warm breeze on the beach
Could it get more perfect?
Is it the weather, or is it my the love in my heart
That provides this cozy effect?

Yellowstone

Bubbling blue lakes that emit a hazy hue
Wandering bison that ignore your every cue
If you are looking for a home away from home,
allow me to show you around Yellowstone.

Even the geysers' predictability will not detract
from the impressive shows you will watch them
enact.
Artificial water shows made at man's hand
could never even dream to be quite this grand.

The wildlife abounds and follows its own
patterns
as if their human spectators have never really
mattered.
Here, natural beauty runs her own stage
and we have the privilege to write about it on
page.

Sounds of mud and water are the things of lore,
like nothing you've heard before
If you think you can imagine it without visiting,
You have no clue what's in store

Overlooking the imminent sulfuric smell,

Yellowstone surpasses the expectations of swell.
I hope to visit again someday
A little slice of paradise awaits my stay.

Strength Rising

It is all over now.
The stress that held you captive
now flees to leave you in peace.
All you need to do now
is re-learn how to breathe.
Inhale deeply and then
exhale with new purpose.
When you push hard enough
barriers give way
and you emerge the victorious one.

I Wanna Write

I wanna write...
I wanna feel the pen glide effortlessly across the paper.
I wanna write a story that encourages people to question their identity.
I wanna write a piece so beautifully crafted that it blows the mind of every individual who reads it and, in turn, leaves them breathless.
I wanna reclaim myself from being Writer's Block's favorite target.
I just wanna let lined paper become my imagination's canvas, painted with dazzling, vivid colors and unique, intricate patterns.
I wanna write a story that appeals to all the young and old inhabitants of this planet.
I wanna write an essay that will bring a sense of unity to all races--this is our world, and we all deal with the same core problems.
I wanna write a poem that will grant me access to every Def Poetry jam.
I wanna write a play that will touch even the most frozen hearts of the coldest people.
I wanna write a novel that, when read by people across the nation, will grant me the title "Einstein of Words".

I wanna write a myriad of meaningful words;
not merely just groups of letters assembled
together, but worlds that contain an unbelievable
amount of insight.
I wanna write an article that gives the whole
truth in nothing less than excruciating detail.
I wanna write what I see, and I wanna write
what I do not know.
I wanna write...

Snapshot of a Prismatic Heart

In the center, purple; the aversion to upset others
by being true to oneself
Zooming out, gold, portraying the love for
others that can turn harmful to the owner of the
heart
Overlapping the gold, red, the passion of
pleasing others; the defect of the former
Pink follows, the childlike joy in the mundane
Green, the need for changes to keep the soul
fresh
Blue, peaceful knowledge that one cannot have a
heart too big

Country Sunset in the Winter

An orange haze above the horizon
a sunset-stained fog
is the evening sky's proclamation
And surrounding the orange, a purplish tint
that conveys serenity
Light refracting through the hues
casts colors into the surrounding fields
and barns and machinery
Frost will soon be settling on the barren fields
that wait for the spring for new purpose
When morning comes, so will new shades
and the crispness of crackling and melting ice

Growing Pains

In a kingdom far far away, a long time ago
There dwelled a young Princess who lived for
the snow
Each flake that landed brought forth a smile
Watching for hours provided escape for a while

But one day it come that the snow went away
And our dear princess did not wish to stay
Her family was stiff; they thought her their
enemy
And upon the spring roses she peered with great
envy

They did not have to fear
They did not have to fight
They were just growing with all of their might

And so the girl knew what she had to do
She worked on her heart and made it anew
Like the beautiful things she strove hard to be
And the sadness that engulfed her fell to its
knees

Horses

Horses are magnificent creatures
Their tails like banners
Their manes like waterfalls
Running hooves sound like thunder

Their tails like banners
As they cut through the wind
Running hooves sound like thunder
From the heavens

As they cut through the wind
They appear as though they're
From the heavens
What a majestic sight to behold

They appear as though their
Manes are like waterfalls
What a majestic sight to behold
Horses are magnificent creatures

Night Stalking

The sky is black and dark
I am not afraid
I hear a coyote's bark
As it continues its nightly raid

I am not afraid
When I see the shifting shape
As it continues its nightly raid
Its appearance like a dark cape

When I see the shifting shape
It turns to look at me and howls
Its appearance like a dark cape
I know it's not just me now

It turns to look at me and howls
I hear a coyote's bark
I know it's not just me now
The sky is black and dark

Anxiety

My mind is still

Like turbulent winds on a blustery day
The kinds that blow rain droplets astray

Still

As a disturbed ocean patch when whales breach
I may appear just peachy but I beseech you

Still

As a yellowjacket roused rudely from sleep
In a passionate fury it causes the nearby to suffer
and weep

Still

My nerves are stable as a derailed train
That skids about a mile before bursting into
flame
Believe me when I say that my existence IS my
bane

So still

My mind is so clear, my anxieties are gone
Actually no, they all jumbled into one
And I can separate myself from none of it

Eyes

He is blind to what others see.
Judging of character
was never his strong suit.
Everyone else sees her fakery but him;
her smirk of a smile,
her overly inflated lips.
People who love him want the best for him
but he is oblivious to what is hidden
behind his perception of her outward beauty.
Everyone wishes he could see her
through their separate eyes.
Otherwise it is feared
he will be trampled upon once again
as always

The Grove

The grove was a mystical place
When the sun shone, it made dew droplets on
the trees glimmer
A pond in its center was always translucent
Fish of shimmering hues mingled and slipped
through the water
The grove attracted me; it drew me in without
fail
How could I stay away from the promise of
magical earthly beauty?
The bridge over the pond provided the perfect
vantage point to view this awesome place
A buzz ran through me each visit; an
overwhelming sense of calm and healing
It exhilarated and invigorated me, a sensation as
real as the stream sliding over the smooth,
rounded rocks
I saw it all clearly and spent hours each day
taking in the sights and all the sounds of
peaceful nature doing what it does best
The grove will always hold a special place in my
memories

Cephalopod

The cephalopod
Eight appendages with mighty strength
An intellectual brain gives it reign of the
undersea landscape
Concealing and revealing itself as it pleases

Eight appendages with mighty strength
It reels in prey with masterful ability
Concealing and revealing itself as it pleases
It outsmarts every aquatic creature

It reels in prey with masterful ability
Better than any trained con artist
It outsmarts every aquatic creature
Three hearts give it incredible stamina

Better than any trained con artist
An intellectual brain gives it reign of the
undersea landscape
Three hearts give it incredible stamina
The cephalopod

A Cozy Afternoon

In our little apartment, we sit next to each other
curled up with blankets and tea
A stormy afternoon, the rain pelts the windows
an auditory familiarity
The cat joins us with a trill, and purrs
with absolute contentment
I reading my book, you playing a game
any stress we feel faces relentment

A Break in Seasonal Depression

Radiant beams soothe my soul
and melt misgivings of the day
Today the mud will not be fed
by relentlessly pelting rain
Like a clock my heart whirrs to life
its gears grinding toward happiness
Where are you, O Strife? I say in my head
this morning I pretend I've never heard of you

Inside, Outside

Glamour, glitter, elegance, and grace
is what I see when I look in her face
But does she see what is behind her?
A majestic, yet ferociously stalking tiger
See, when life becomes easy, we become
self-focused
and do not see clearly outside
So now I fear that if no one is near,
she may be attacked and die

The Dreamer

A blanket of silence falls upon the sleepy house
Everyone is asleep or at least well on their way
to dreamland
That is, all but one
Late at night, her mind remains inspired
and her pondering thoughts, pen, paper,
and language all collaborate
Her pen strokes the paper by lamplight,
a dim and dreamy display of formed letters with
a romantic glow
The girl's mind probes for just the right words
and phrases
Every line must be carefully crafted, formations
selected with exclusivity
She longs to create something that dazzles
While her surroundings are dark and quiet,
her mind buzzes vividly, alert
But it is late
Reluctantly she caps her favorite pen
and returns her journal to bed

The Bush and the Flower

A bush, a flower
in this tender hour
So unassuming
therefore the world scours
them of their emotional beauty
Forgetting the artistry of creation
might as well be the cremation
of joy and happiness,
now devoid of expectations
for life as we know it

The creatures that dwell inside
they scurry and hide
but sometimes show off their colors
The birds so flashy
The insect so sly
And spiders that weave
but don't close your eyes
lest you miss natures glorious disguise

While the world keeps booming
about it's wild pace
We have forgotten nature's place;
Of contemplative yearning

growing and learning
To have peace with the Creator
whom we all meet sooner or later

July 4th

It was a warm evening with a comfortable
breeze
my best friend came over with her family
for a 4th of July barbeque at our house
In the backyard we gathered
while our fathers grilled classic beef franks
I, being a quirky little kid
had printed off the lyrics
for the Addam's Family theme song
for my friend and I to commit to memory
and then perform for our younger siblings and
parents
We memorized it as we swung on the swing set
in the backyard playground
that my dad had built for my sister and I
Our two younger sisters had found the garden
cart
and were taking turns riding down the grassy hill
in our backyard atop it, using the handle to steer
Later on, on a July 4th several years later,
we would convince our 80-year-old grandmother
to do the same, and she enjoyed the ride
When the food was ready
we reluctantly gave up our activities
but had built up quite the appetite

Hotdogs never tasted so good
I remember this day often

An Ode to the Elephant

25

Elephants
Gray and textured skin
Perceptive and wise
Trunks of great dexterity

Gray and textured skin
Leathery and weathered with life
Trunks of great dexterity
With eyes that pierce intentions

Leathery and weathered with life
They spend their days with family
With eyes that pierce intentions
As they travel together ponderously

They spend their days with family
Perceptive and wise
As they travel together ponderously
Elephants

To Stand Up for Myself

I've been pushed and kicked
Knocked over and nicked
Assumed I'd do something I wouldn't

Far too long to be a doormat
Time for me to say "no more of that"
And learn to stand up for myself

I love to help others, but at what cost?
To the point that I feel lost
And no longer know what I want?

That is not me anymore